Pip Sips

By Sally Cowan

Tam sits.

Tam sips.

Pip sips.

Sip, sip, sip!

Sit, Pip, sit!

CHECKING FOR MEANING

1. What does Tam do? *(Literal)*

2. Whose drink does Pip sip? *(Literal)*

3. How do you think Tam is feeling at the end of the story? *(Inferential)*

EXTENDING VOCABULARY

Tam	Look at the word *Tam.* What is the first sound in this word? What other words can you think of that begin with this sound?
sips	Look at the word *sips.* What is the base of this word? What has been added to the base? Can you think of another word that means the same as *sips*?
sip	Look at the word *sip.* Can you think of other words that rhyme with *sip*?

MOVING BEYOND THE TEXT

1. Why do you think Tam was sitting outside?

2. What are some other reasons why people drink or eat outside?

3. What do rabbits normally eat and drink?

4. What do you think Tam did next?

SPEED SOUNDS

| Mm | Ss | Aa | Pp | Ii | Tt |

PRACTICE WORDS

sits

Tam

sips

sip

Pip

sit

mat

Sit